perfect
# puddings

# perfect puddings

## tessa bramley

### photography by christine hanscomb

RYLAND
PETERS
& SMALL
LONDON NEW YORK

| | |
|---|---|
| **Designer** | Luis Peral-Aranda |
| **Commissioning Editor** | Elsa Petersen-Schepelern |
| **Editors** | Siobhan O'Connor |
| | Maddalena Bastianelli |
| **Production** | Patricia Harrington |
| **Art Director** | Gabriella Le Grazie |
| **Publishing Director** | Alison Starling |
| | |
| **Food Stylist** | Maxine Clark |
| **Stylist** | Antonia Gaunt |
| **Photographer's Assistant** | Teresa Cotterell |

First published in Great Britain in 2002
by Ryland Peters & Small
Kirkman House
12–14 Whitfield Street
London W1T 2RP
www.rylandpeters.com

10 9 8 7 6 5 4 3 2

Text © Tessa Bramley 2002
Design and photographs
© Ryland Peters & Small 2002

ISBN 1 84172 283 9

Printed and bound in China

## Dedication and Acknowledgements

I dedicate this book with special thanks to my brother, Howard, whose love of puddings is legendary and whose sweet tooth inspired me. I hope you like it Howard.

Thanks to my mum whose pastry was exemplary, to Andrew, Carole and Linda who believe in me and support me and of course, posthumously, to Sarah, my grandma, who set me on the right track all those years ago. My thanks to Nathan and Caroline for testing and tasting the recipes and to Andrew for keeping things ticking over whilst we played! I am indebted to Elsa at Ryland Peters & Small for patiently urging me on, for her boundless enthusiasm for the subject and for producing such a lovely book.

## Notes

All spoon measurements are level unless otherwise stated.

All eggs are medium, unless otherwise specified. Uncooked or partly cooked eggs should not be served to the very young, the very old, those with compromised immune systems, or to pregnant women.

Preheat ovens to the specified temperature. These recipes were tested with a regular oven. If using a fan-assisted oven, decrease the cooking times according to the manufacturer's instructions.

Recipes in this book were tested using best quality cooking chocolate, 55–60 per cent cocoa solids. To melt chocolate, put it into a heatproof bowl set over a saucepan of simmering water. Do not let the water touch the base of the bowl. Melt gently – do not let any water or steam touch the chocolate, or it will turn into an unusable lump.

Recipes in this book use whole vanilla pods or best quality vanilla extract. Do not use cheap vanilla essence, which will not give the correct flavour. Vanilla pods, though expensive, can be reused, even after they have been split and the seeds removed. Just dry them off with kitchen paper and store in an airtight jar of caster sugar or icing sugar. The resulting vanilla flavoured sugar may then be used in recipes.

**Sterilizing preserving jars** Wash the jars in hot, soapy water and rinse in boiling water. Put into a large saucepan and cover with hot water. With the lid on, bring the water to the boil and continue boiling for 15 minutes. Turn off the heat, then leave the jars in the hot water until just before they are to be filled. Invert the jars onto a clean cloth to dry. Sterilize the lids for 5 minutes, by boiling or according to the manufacturer's instructions. The jars should be filled and sealed while they are still hot. For useful guidelines on preserving, see website http://hgic.clemson.edu/factsheets/HGIC3040.htm.

# contents

# the perfect finale ...

A pudding is an unequivocal luxury. It takes time and loving care to make. Intensely fruity, luscious and creamy, or buttery and gloriously decadent, puddings and self indulgence go hand in hand.

When she was young, my grandma, Sarah, was a parlourmaid in a grand Victorian household. She always taught me that puddings should be lavishly produced from the best ingredients – she firmly believed in the 'wow!' factor. From her I learned about spices and flavourings, about the importance of using unsalted butter for baking (she would call it 'sweet' butter), and about serving puddings with a flourish. It was the proud gleam in her eye when she presented her wonderful pear and almond tart which added to its enjoyment: it was a simple presentation, just pure ground almonds with a beautiful sticky glaze, yet a sublime experience.

She showed me how to take pleasure in the feel and scent of ingredients – that the purest flavour of a lemon is in the oil of the zest. We spent some happy mornings rubbing the lemon skins all over with sugar lumps to extract the intense flavour, all ready to make her famous lemon curd before baking day started. The sugar acted as a very fine grater, removing the surface lemon colour, tinting the sugar yellow and at the same time absorbing the lemon oil to give the curd we made with it a clear and zingy citrus tang.

Some of the puddings in this book are outrageously luxurious, while others are simple and homely – all are created with love for you to enjoy.

real
puddings

Very simple, very light and impossible to resist, this nursery pudding has always been one of the most popular we have ever served at The Old Vicarage. To 'gild the lily', I like to top each one with a chocolate heart. The chocolate melts into the hot fudge sauce, leaving a pale, matte impression on the glossy surface. Easy and stylish for a special occasion.

# baked chocolate pudding
## with chocolate fudge sauce and custard

185 g self-raising flour

1 teaspoon baking powder

½ teaspoon bicarbonate of soda

2 heaped tablespoons cocoa powder

150 g caster sugar

2 extra large eggs, beaten

2 tablespoons golden syrup

200 ml milk

200 ml sunflower oil

Chocolate fudge sauce

175 g extra bitter dark chocolate

250 ml double cream

250 g icing sugar, sifted

To serve

Chocolate Hearts (optional)*

hot Quick Vanilla Custard (see page 62), hot

*8 small pudding moulds, 175 ml each, greased*

Serves 8

To make the pudding, sieve the flour, baking powder, bicarbonate of soda, cocoa powder and caster sugar into a mixing bowl. Make a well in the centre. Pour the beaten eggs into the well, then add the golden syrup, milk and oil. Using a whisk, gradually draw in the dry ingredients from the sides of the bowl and beat to make a smooth batter.

Pour the mixture into the prepared moulds and bake in a preheated oven at 150°C (300°F) Gas 2 for about 30 minutes, until springy to the touch.

To make the fudge sauce, put the chocolate and cream into the top of a double boiler and melt gently over a medium heat. Alternatively, use a heatproof bowl set over a saucepan of steaming water. Gradually beat in the icing sugar until the sauce is glossy and all the sugar has dissolved.

To serve, unmould the puddings onto small plates and pour the hot custard around the puddings. Pour the fudge sauce over the top and serve immediately.

**Chocolate Hearts** Put about 50 g dark chocolate into a heatproof bowl set over a saucepan of simmering water. Do not let the water touch the base of the bowl. Heat until melted. Pour the melted chocolate onto a sheet of baking parchment and let it set. Cut out little heart shapes using a petits fours cutter. Put one on top of each pudding just before serving. The hot fudge sauce will melt the heart, leaving a slightly lighter impression on top of the pudding.

*A very light, fresh and lemony pudding with a zingy lemon sauce – it couldn't be simpler. I think it's even better with a little puddle of homemade custard (page 62), but then I am a custard fan!*

# baked lemon pudding
## with lemon butter sauce

175 g self-raising flour

1½ teaspoons baking powder

a pinch of salt

175 g caster sugar

finely grated zest of 2 lemons

3 eggs, beaten

175 g unsalted butter, melted, then cooled

3 drops of lemon oil

75 ml milk mixed with 75 ml cold water

Quick Candied Lemon Zest, to serve (optional)*

Lemon butter sauce

6 tablespoons caster sugar

finely grated zest and juice of 2 lemons, plus the juice of 1 extra lemon

2 tablespoons Cointreau

100 g unsalted butter, cut into cubes and chilled

*6 individual pudding tins, greased, then dredged with a mixture of flour and caster sugar*

Serves 6

To make the pudding, sieve the flour, baking powder, salt and sugar into a bowl and stir in the zest. Make a well in the centre and add the eggs, butter, lemon oil and milk mixture. Mix with a small whisk to form a smooth batter.

Pour into the prepared tins and bake in a preheated oven at 180°C (350°F) Gas 4 for about 20–25 minutes, until well risen and golden. The puddings should feel as firm in the middle as they do at the sides. Turn the tins upside down onto a wire cooling rack and let cool for 5 minutes. Ease a small knife around the sides of the tins to loosen each pudding, then gently shake out.

To make the sauce, put the sugar and lemon juice into a small, non-reactive (stainless steel or enamel) saucepan and dissolve gently over a low heat. Add the lemon zest and bring to the boil. Cook at a fast bubble for 2–3 minutes to reduce the liquid to a thick syrup. Remove from the heat and strain out the zest. Add the Cointreau, then whisk in the chilled butter, a little at a time, until the sauce is thickened and glossy.

Serve with the sauce poured over and around each pudding. A little pile of candied zest on top adds crunch and tangy freshness.

**\*Quick Candied Lemon Zest**  Using a lemon zester or cannelle knife, remove long, fine strips of zest from 1 lemon. Put into a saucepan of cold water and bring to the boil to soften the strips. Drain, then dry the zest with kitchen paper. Transfer to a small saucepan, add 2 tablespoons caster sugar and toss over the heat until the sugar has stuck to the lemon and formed a candied coating. Store in a little box of sugar until needed.

Choose your favourite berries or stone fruit for this orange sponge pudding. The recipe can change with the seasons – although I think the deep purple of blueberries and blackberries make a particularly attractive pudding. I used blueberries and cherries this time, but would avoid strawberries.

# blueberry and cherry sponge pudding

500 g mixed fruit such as pitted cherries and blueberries

125 g caster sugar, plus 3 tablespoons extra

125 g self-raising flour

a pinch of salt

1 teaspoon baking powder

125 g unsalted butter, softened

2 large eggs, lightly beaten

finely grated zest of 1 orange

hot Quick Vanilla Custard (see page 62) or cream, to serve

*1.2 litre pudding bowl, greased, then dredged with a mixture of plain flour and caster sugar*

Serves 6–8

Reserve 125 ml of the fruit and 1 tablespoon of the sugar. Mix the remaining fruit with 2 tablespoons of the sugar, then transfer to the prepared pudding bowl.

Sieve the flour, salt and baking powder into a second bowl.

Put the softened butter and remaining 125 g caster sugar into a mixing bowl and beat until very light, fluffy and creamy in colour. Add the eggs, a little at a time, beating between each addition, until the mixture is light and fluffy. Add the orange zest.

Sieve half the flour mixture over the butter mixture and lightly fold in the flour with a metal spoon. Repeat with the remaining flour, taking care not to over-mix: the mixture should drop softly off the spoon. If it is too stiff, fold in about 1 tablespoon water to make a soft dropping consistency.

Spoon the mixture over the fruit, starting at the edges and working towards the centre. Smooth the top, making a slight indentation with the spoon in the middle so the mixture will rise evenly.

Bake in a preheated oven at 180°C (350°F) Gas 4 for 30–35 minutes until golden, well risen and as firm in the middle as it is at the sides. Remove from the oven and let settle a little before turning out onto a serving dish.

To make the sauce, put the reserved fruit and sugar into a blender and blend to a smooth purée. Serve the pudding with sauce and cream or custard.

# apricot bread and butter puddings

Light and wobbly bread and butter pudding is true nursery food. Rather than the more usual dried fruits, I prefer to use tangy apricots, which I think counterbalance the creaminess of the custard. Served with a sharp, fresh apricot sauce, this homely pudding makes an altogether more elegant dish, fit for a dinner party.

**1 vanilla pod, split lengthways and seeds scraped out**

**450 ml milk**

**450 ml double cream**

**5 large free range eggs**

**125 g caster sugar**

**grated zest of 1 lemon**

**unsalted butter, for spreading**

**8 slices brioche**

**6–8 no-need-to-soak dried apricots, chopped**

**a sprinkling of brown sugar, for topping**

Apricot purée

**250 g pitted fresh apricots or 150 g no-need-to-soak dried apricots**

**juice of 1 lemon**

**125 g caster sugar**

**1 tablespoon apricot brandy or brandy**

*6 small ovenproof dishes or 1 large dish, about 15 cm x 20 cm x 7.5 cm deep*

*a baking sheet*

Serves 6

To make the custard, put the milk, cream and vanilla pod and seeds into a large saucepan and bring to the boil.

Put the eggs and sugar into a large bowl and whisk until frothy. Whisk the vanilla cream into the eggs: the mixture will start to thicken lightly. Stir in the lemon zest.

Lightly butter the brioche. Arrange half the brioche, butter side up, in the dishes. Sprinkle half the chopped apricots over the top. Gently pour the custard over the top, letting it soak into the brioche. Sprinkle with the remaining apricots, top with the rest of the brioche, butter side up, and gently pour in the remaining custard, so that it comes to the top of the dishes.

Stand the dishes on a baking sheet (which is easier to lift in and out of the oven) and cook in a preheated oven at 120°C (250°F) Gas 1 for 45 minutes, until the custard is just set but still slightly wobbly.

Meanwhile, to make the purée, put the fresh apricots into a saucepan, add the lemon juice, sugar, brandy and about 4 tablespoons water and simmer until the fruit has softened, about 10–15 minutes. Transfer to a blender and purée until smooth. Taste and add extra lemon juice or sugar to taste. The amount of water will depend on how juicy the fruits are – if the purée looks too thick, add a little more. (If using dried apricots, increase the amount of water to 150 ml.)

Remove the puddings from the oven, sprinkle with the brown sugar and brown under a preheated grill or with a blowtorch, until the top caramelizes to a crisp golden brown. Serve with the apricot purée.

# coffee hazelnut pudding
## with coffee bean sauce

Coffee and hazelnuts make a delicious marriage of flavors. You might also like to serve it with a simple orange compote (below).

**60 g shelled hazelnuts**

**60 g self-raising flour**

**½ teaspoon baking powder**

**a pinch of salt**

**120 g unsalted butter, softened**

**120 g brown sugar**

**finely grated zest of 1 orange**

**2 teaspoons liquid instant coffee**

**2 eggs, beaten**

Coffee bean sauce

**225 g caster sugar**

**125 ml strong black coffee made with freshly ground beans, such as a mixture of Costa Rica and Java**

**5 tablespoons double cream**

To serve (optional)

**a few coffee beans**

**1–2 tablespoons malt whisky**

**candied orange zest, to serve (variation on Quick Candied Lemon Zest, page 10)**

*4 individual pudding basins, 150 ml each, buttered and base-lined with greaseproof paper*

Serves 4

To make the pudding, put the hazelnuts into a blender and grind until chunky. Transfer to a bowl, then stir in the flour, baking powder and salt.

Put the butter, sugar, orange zest and coffee into a second bowl and beat until light and fluffy (use an electric mixer if you have one). Gradually whisk the eggs into the mixture. Carefully fold in the flour mixture until evenly mixed. It should have a soft dropping consistency. Divide the batter between the prepared pudding basins and bake in a preheated oven at 160°C (325°F) Gas 3 for about 25 minutes, or until well risen and firm to the touch.

Meanwhile, to make the coffee bean sauce, put the sugar into a saucepan, add 5 tablespoons water and dissolve over a low heat. As the liquid becomes clear, increase the heat and bring to the boil. Cook, without stirring, until the sugar forms a golden caramel. Remove from the heat and carefully pour over the coffee (the caramel will splutter, so protect your hand with a cloth). Return to the heat and add the cream. Continue stirring until the mixture is smooth, then let simmer until reduced to a coating consistency. Remove from the heat, then add the coffee beans and whisky to taste.

Run a little knife around the puddings and turn out carefully onto serving plates. Pour the sauce over and around, and serve with the orange compote. If you like, you can garnish the puddings with candied orange zest (see page 10).

**Orange Compote** Put the zest of 2 oranges into a saucepan, cover with water and bring to the boil. Drain. Cut out the orange segments. Put 4 tablespoons sugar into a saucepan, add 4 tablespoons water and simmer until reduced by half. Add the drained zest and orange segments, and chill until ready to serve.

# pies and tarts

# old fashioned
# **apple and cinnamon pie**

What could be better than a simple apple pie, with delicious, crisp pie crust and spicy sweet apples, just hot from the oven?

**2 recipes Old Vic Foolproof Pastry (page 63)**

Apple filling

**2 teaspoons semolina or fine cornmeal**

**675 g cooking apples, about 4 large, peeled, cored and fairly thickly sliced**

**4 tablespoons caster sugar, plus extra for sprinkling**

**2 cinnamon sticks, broken into 2–3 pieces to release the flavour**

**whipped cream or ice cream, to serve (optional)**

*a deep pie dish, 25 cm diameter*

Serves 4

Prepare the pastry, cover with clingfilm and chill in the refrigerator for about 1 hour. Cut off just a little less than half the pastry, roll out and use to line the base of the pie dish. Sprinkle with the semolina: this mops up the excess juices from the fruit, making a sauce that prevents the pastry becoming soggy. Cover and refrigerate the remaining pastry until ready to use.

Fill the lined pie dish with layers of apple, sprinkling sugar and cinnamon between the layers. You will have lots of fruit, but use it all – mound it up in the centre of the dish, because the apples will fall during baking. The aim is a very full, generous-looking finished pie.

Roll out the remaining pastry, lift carefully using the rolling pin and gently ease it over the fruit, taking care not to stretch the pastry. Moisten the edges with water and press the pastry onto the bottom layer around the edge of the dish. Trim off any excess with a sharp knife. Knock the edges together with the back of a knife, then pinch or flute the edges together with your fingers or a fork. Using kitchen scissors, snip the top of the pie in several places to let the steam escape as it cooks.

Bake in a preheated oven at 200°C (400°F) Gas 6 for 25 minutes to crisp the pastry, then lower the temperature to 190°C (375°F) Gas 5 and bake for a further 40–50 minutes, until the pastry and fruit are cooked through (you will need to test it with a skewer). After the first 30 minutes, you can gently rest a piece of folded baking parchment over the pie to stop it browning too much.

As soon as you take it from the oven, sprinkle with caster sugar so it sticks to the hot pastry. Let cool a little, then serve with cream or ice cream.

# caramelized apple tartlets

French apple tarts always look very stylish and are scrummy to eat. It's a good idea to use dessert apples for the topping because they hold their shape better and don't need much extra sugar.

1 recipe Old Vic Foolproof Pastry (page 63)

½ recipe Pastry Cream (page 26)

icing sugar, for dusting

tiny fresh bay leaves, to serve (optional)

Apple purée

2 large cooking apples, about 500 g, peeled, cored and sliced

1½ tablespoons caster sugar

1 strip of lemon zest

1 tablespoon Calvados

Apple topping

1 tablespoon caster sugar

1 tablespoon unsalted butter

4 red apples, peeled, cored and thinly sliced*

*a loose-based fluted tart tin, 20 cm diameter, or 6 tartlet tins, 10 cm diameter*

*foil and baking beans or uncooked rice*

Serves 6

To make the apple purée, put the apples into a saucepan, add the sugar, lemon zest and 2 tablespoons water, bring to the boil and simmer until cooked to a thick, dry purée. Add the Calvados and taste for sweetness, adding a little more sugar if necessary. Chill until needed.

Meanwhile, make the pastry and roll out on a floured surface to about 5 mm thick. Cut the pastry into 6, line the tins and chill as described on page 63.

Line with foil and fill with baking beans or uncooked rice. Bake in a preheated oven at 200°C (400°F) Gas 6 for about 15 minutes. (This is called baking blind.) Remove the foil and beans, lower the oven temperature to 180°C (350°F) Gas 4 and return the pastry case to the oven for a further 5 minutes, until the pastry is cooked through. Increase the oven temperature to 220°C (425°F) Gas 7.

To make the apple topping, heat 1 tablespoon water in a small saucepan and add the sugar and butter. Bring to the boil. Add the apple slices and cook for 2–3 minutes, until softened slightly and coated with the buttery syrup.

Divide the pastry cream between the tartlets and top with 1 tablespoon of the apple purée. Arrange overlapping apple slices on top of the apple purée to cover the surface completely. Bake in the preheated oven for 7–8 minutes, until the edges of the apple slices are deep golden and caramelized. Lightly dredge with icing sugar, top with a tiny bay leaf and serve.

*Note  The large tart uses 4 apples, the tartlets use 3.

A fabulous yet simple alternative to the classic lemon meringue pie. I use dessert apples which break down to a coarse purée, because I prefer to have some texture in the filling. You could, of course, use cooking apples, but then you must increase the sugar in the purée. If you don't like cardamom, use three or four cloves instead, but remove after making the filling.

# apple amber

1 recipe Old Vic Foolproof Pastry (page 63)

8 large dessert apples, peeled, cored and chopped

3 strips of lemon zest and freshly squeezed juice of ½ lemon

seeds from 12 crushed green cardamom pods

2–3 tablespoons caster sugar, or to taste (leave slightly tart because of the sweetness of the meringue)

3 large egg yolks

Meringue topping

3 large egg whites

a pinch of salt

375 g caster sugar, plus extra for sprinkling

2 teaspoons cornflour

2 teaspoons lemon juice

*a loose-based flan tin, 20 cm diameter*

*foil and baking beans or uncooked rice*

Serves 8–10

Make the pastry, use to line the flan tin and bake blind as described on page 63. Let cool while you make the filling. Reduce the oven temperature to 110°C (225°F) Gas ¼. (Make sure the oven has cooled down to this temperature before completing baking.)

To make the filling, put the apples, lemon zest and juice, cardamom seeds, sugar and 3 tablespoons water into a saucepan and cook over moderate heat until softened to a coarse pulp. Remove and discard the strips of lemon zest.

Put the 3 egg yolks into a bowl, beat well, then stir into the apple purée. Pour the mixture into the cooked and cooled pastry case.

To make the meringue topping, put the egg whites and salt into a clean, dry bowl and whisk until stiff. Whisk in 1 tablespoon of the sugar until the mixture is glossy and standing in stiff peaks. Whisk in the remaining sugar in 2 batches, whisking back to stiff peaks after each addition. Sprinkle with the cornflour and lemon juice and fold in gently (I like to use the whisk for this).

Using a large spoon, pile the meringue on top of the apple filling. Sprinkle about 1 tablespoon sugar over the top. Bake in the cool oven for about 1 hour until the meringue is crisp on the outside with the peaks just tinged golden. The centre of the meringue will be fluffy and marshmallow-like.

# pear and almond frangipane tart

A tart that looks spectacular, but is simple and inexpensive to make. You could use almost any kind of fruit – it also works well with plums and fresh apricots. With its light texture, it's best eaten on the day it's made, but does freeze very well. However, do serve it warm.

**1 recipe Old Vic Foolproof Pastry (page 63)**
**6 tablespoons apricot jam**
**125 g unsalted butter, softened**
**125 g caster sugar**
**2 eggs, beaten**
**1 tablespoon self-raising flour**
**1 teaspoon baking powder**
**125 g ground almonds or 175 blanched almonds, ground in a blender**

Following the recipe on page 63, make the pastry, use to line the prepared flan tin and bake blind. Remove from the oven and let the pastry cool, but keep the oven at 180°C (350°F) Gas 4.

Spread about 2½ tablespoons of the jam into the cooked pastry case. Put the remaining 3½ tablespoons into a small saucepan, add 2–3 tablespoons water and bring to the boil. Sieve to remove any pieces of fruit. (This is the glaze for painting the tart before serving.)

Put the butter and sugar into a bowl, then beat until light and fluffy. Add the beaten eggs, a little at a time, beating well until the mixture is very light.

**3 almost ripe pears,
peeled, halved and cored**

*a rectangular loose-based flan tin,
33 x 9 cm, or a round flan tin,
28 cm diameter*

*foil and baking beans
or uncooked rice*

Serves 4–6

Sieve the flour and baking powder into a separate bowl and stir in the ground almonds. Fold the flour mixture lightly into the butter mixture – it will drop softly off the spoon. Spread evenly over the jam in the pastry case.

Put the pear halves cut side down onto a chopping board. With a sharp knife, slice the pears lengthways, leaving the stem end still intact. Press down on the fruit with the flat of your hand so the slices fan out. Using a spatula or palette knife, lift the pear fans onto the tart. Arrange the stem ends towards the centre if using a round tin, or set alternately, top to tail, if using a rectangular tin.

Bake in the preheated oven for 40–50 minutes until the almond filling is well risen and feels firm in the middle. To test, insert a skewer inserted into the almond filling: it should come out clean. Brush with the apricot glaze and serve warm.

# raspberry tart with caramel almonds

A spectacular dinner party finale with a shortbread crust. The caramel shards add special drama, but, for a more homely occasion, omit them and fill the space with more raspberries.

125 g unsalted butter
60 g caster sugar
125 g plain flour
60 g semolina
500 g raspberries

Caramel almond shards
10 blanched almonds, chopped
140 g caster sugar

Pastry cream
4 egg yolks
2 tablespoons plain flour
1 teaspoon cornflour
2 tablespoons caster sugar
600 ml single cream
1 vanilla pod, split lengthways and seeds scraped out
1 tablespoon ground almonds
1 tablespoon framboise (raspberry) liqueur, or brandy

*a baking sheet, lined with baking parchment*

*a loose-based flan tin, 25 cm diameter*

*foil and baking beans or uncooked rice*

Serves 4–6

To make the shortbread pastry, put the butter and sugar into a bowl and beat until creamy. Put the flour and semolina into a second bowl and mix well. Gradually beat in the butter mixture to form a crumbly dough. Transfer to a floured work surface and knead carefully until it comes together smoothly. As described in the recipe on page 62, roll out to line the flan tin, chill for 1 hour, then bake blind in a preheated oven at 150°C (300°F) Gas 2 for 20 minutes. Let cool.

To make the caramel almond shards, sprinkle the prepared baking sheet with the chopped nuts. Put the sugar into a heavy-based saucepan, add 3 tablespoons water and heat gently until the sugar dissolves. Boil rapidly until it forms a golden caramel. Pour over the nuts and let cool completely. When cold and set, gently tap the caramel and break it into shards. Reserve.

To make the pastry cream, put the egg yolks, flour, cornflour and sugar into a bowl and whisk until blended. Put the cream into a saucepan, add the vanilla pod and seeds and bring to the boil. Pour the hot cream onto the egg mixture, and whisk vigorously.

Pour into a bowl, rinse the saucepan, return the mixture to the pan and cook gently over low heat, stirring all the time until it thickly coats the back of a spoon.

Remove and discard the vanilla pod and stir in the ground almonds and liqueur. Pour the pastry cream into the cooked pastry case. Let cool completely.

When cool, arrange the raspberries neatly on top of the pastry cream, leaving the centre clear. Pile the centre of the tart with the glossy shards of caramelized almonds. Serve.

*A deliciously rich yet fragile pastry that must be well chilled before you attempt to roll it out. I make the pastry the day before I need it and keep it in the refrigerator. The semolina thickens the fruit juices during baking, making a lovely syrupy sauce.*

# blackberry, apple and orange deep dish pie

75 g full-fat cream cheese

75 g unsalted butter, softened

125 g plain flour

**Fruit filling**

1 tablespoon unsalted butter

500 g Granny Smith apples, peeled, cored and sliced

2 tablespoons semolina

6 tablespoons caster sugar

grated zest and juice of 3 oranges

500 g blackberries or loganberries

icing sugar, for dusting

**Orange crème fraîche (optional)**

250 ml crème fraîche

2 teaspoons icing sugar

grated zest of 1 orange

*an oval or round deep pie dish, about 20 cm diameter*

Serves 6

To make the pastry, put the cream cheese and butter into a bowl and beat until light and fluffy. Add the flour gradually, beating into the dough until it is well blended. Wrap in clingfilm and chill until needed.

To make the filling, dice the butter, put into a large saucepan and heat until melted. Add the apple slices, turning them in the butter to coat. Put the semolina onto a plate. Remove the apples from the pan and toss in the semolina.

Put the sugar, orange zest and juice and 1 tablespoon water into a saucepan, bring to the boil, then reduce to a syrup. Put the apples into the pie dish, add the blackberries and mix gently. Pour over the orange syrup and let cool.

Put the pastry onto a lightly floured work top. Roll out carefully and evenly to a shape about 2.5 cm larger than the top of the pie dish. Cut to shape and use the trimmings to make a thin layer round the top edge of the dish. Moisten with a little water.

Using the rolling pin to help you, ease the pastry over the top of the dish. Press the edges of the 2 layers of pastry firmly together. Either crimp or flute the edge of the pastry using your fingers. Make several vents in the top of the pastry lid to let the steam escape as the pie cooks.

Bake in a preheated oven at 190°C (375°F) Gas 5 for 25 minutes until the pastry is golden brown and the fruit is tender. (Test with a skewer through the vents in the crust.) Let cool slightly and dust with sifted icing sugar. Mix the crème fraîche with the sugar and orange zest and serve with the pie.

# key lime pie

The American classic key lime pie is made with a graham cracker or cookie crumb crust and topped with whipped cream. My version has a brûlée-style topping and uses my favourite pastry base from the restaurant. You need a deep pastry case to make this tart successfully. When baking blind, put in enough baking beans to come well up the sides, to prevent the pastry shrinking back in the tin. The crisp coating hides a velvety smooth and delicate custard with a zingy fresh lime flavour. Use a thin, very sharp knife to cut it, inserting the point first.

**250 g Old Vic Foolproof Pastry (page 63)**

**1 egg white, for brushing**

Lime filling

**6 free range eggs**

**350 g caster sugar**

**finely grated zest and freshly squeezed juice of 10 key limes or 4 regular limes, about 125 ml**

**500 ml double cream**

**icing sugar, for dusting**

*a fluted flan tin, 22 cm diameter, 5 cm deep*

*foil and baking beans or uncooked rice*

Serves 6

Make the pastry, line the flan tin and bake blind in a preheated oven as described on page 63. While still warm, brush the inside of the pastry case with the beaten egg white, then let cool completely. This will seal the pastry and keep it crisp when filled. Reduce the oven temperature to 140°C (275°F) Gas 1.

To make the lime custard filling, put the eggs and sugar into a bowl and whisk well. Add the grated lime zest and juice. Stir in the cream and chill for 30 minutes.

Strain the lime custard through a fine sieve and discard the residue. Carefully pour the custard into the cooked pastry case, filling right to the top of the crust. Transfer to the oven and bake for 1–1¼ hours, until the custard is just about set. It will still be slightly wobbly and will continue to set as it cools. Let cool completely on a wire rack.

Transfer to a serving platter and dredge the top thickly with icing sugar. Using a blowtorch, apply direct heat to the sugar until it melts and caramelizes to a deep golden colour. When cold, this will form a thin, crisp sugar glaze. A similar effect can be achieved by caramelizing under a hot grill, but you must cover the pastry edge with foil to prevent it burning.

# crumbles, cobblers and betties

Brown betties were very popular in country kitchens during the 19th century. The traditional recipe used apples, but I like the stickiness of the plum juices better.

## plum and nutmeg
# brown betty

140 g brown sugar

600 g ripe, sweet, juicy plums, halved and pitted

grated zest and juice of 2 limes

½ nutmeg, freshly grated, plus extra, to serve

85 g unsalted butter

165 g fresh brown breadcrumbs

Quick Vanilla Custard (page 62) or cream, to serve

*an ovenproof dish, about 25 cm diameter, greased*

Serves 4–6

Reserve 1 tablespoon of the sugar and put the remainder into a bowl. Add the plums, lime zest and juice, grated nutmeg and 1 tablespoon water. Mix well. Set aside to soak for about 30 minutes, so the sugar and plums make lots of juice.

Put the butter into a heavy-based frying pan, melt gently, then add the breadcrumbs. Cook over medium heat, stirring constantly with a wooden spoon, until all the butter has been absorbed and the crumbs are golden.

Arrange the fruit and crumbs in layers in the prepared dish, finishing with a layer of crumbs. Press down with the back of a spoon to compact the topping, then rough up with a fork and sprinkle with the reserved sugar.

Bake in the middle of a preheated oven at 190°C (375°F) Gas 5 for about 45 minutes, until the plums are tender and the top is crispy and brown. (Test the plums with a skewer.)

Serve with custard or cream, sprinkled with a little extra grated nutmeg.

# apple cobbler with pecans and maple syrup

The flavours of maple syrup and pecan nuts marry beautifully in this simple pudding. It's important to use a pure, thick maple syrup to give a distinctive toffee flavour. Lighter syrups are certainly cheaper to buy, but bear little resemblance to the real thing.

1 kg crisp red apples, peeled, cored and thinly sliced

45 g unsalted butter

1 vanilla pod, split lengthways and seeds scraped out

180 g shelled pecan halves

4 tablespoons pure maple syrup

Quick Vanilla Custard (page 62), to serve

Cobbler topping

200 g self-raising flour

½ teaspoon salt

3 teaspoons baking powder

50 g unsalted butter, cut into small pieces

50 g rolled oats, plus 1 tablespoon extra

1 tablespoon caster sugar

150 ml skimmed milk

1 egg

a little cream or milk, to glaze

1 tablespoon brown sugar

*an ovenproof baking dish, about 25 cm diameter, 5 cm deep*

Serves 6–8

Put the prepared apples into a saucepan, add the butter, 5 tablespoons water and the vanilla pod and its seeds. Simmer over a low heat until the juices start to flow and the apples soften, about 10 minutes.

Remove from the heat, then stir in the pecans and syrup. Pour into the baking dish and let cool. Before adding the topping, remove the vanilla pod.

To make the topping, sieve the flour, salt and baking powder into a large bowl. Add the butter and rub in with your fingertips until there are no lumps of butter left and the mixture looks like fine breadcrumbs. Stir in the oats and sugar and make a well in the centre. Put the milk and egg into a second bowl and beat well. Add to the well in the flour and oat mixture. Using a table knife, draw the mixture lightly together to form a soft dough.

Turn out onto a floured work surface and lightly knead the dough until smooth underneath. Form into a round shape and press out gently with the flat of your hand to about 1½ cm thick. Using a sharp knife, cut the circle in half, then into 6 or 8 wedges. Arrange on top of the fruit with the points facing inward. Brush with a little cream or milk, then sprinkle with the extra oats and brown sugar.

Bake in a preheated oven at 220°C (425°F) Gas 7 for 5 minutes. Reduce the heat to 200°C (400°F) Gas 6 and bake for a further 17–20 minutes, or until a skewer inserted into the topping comes out clean. The cobbler should look well risen, crunchy and golden brown. Serve with vanilla custard.

Rhubarb crumble was one of my grandma's favourites and we ate it warm with custard. Although not, strictly speaking, a crumble, it had a beautifully crisp topping, which we all adored. She used to grow rhubarb in her kitchen garden and would always 'force' some under upturned buckets to use in early spring. I loved pulling the long, bright pink stems from the crowns. We would make cones of greaseproof paper, fill them with sugar, then dip in the slender rhubarb stems and nibble them. If you're not a fan of ginger, try finely grated orange zest instead. The two flavours work equally well with rhubarb.

# rhubarb crumble
## with gingered vanilla

**675 g forced rhubarb**

**3 pieces of crystallized ginger**

**115 g caster sugar**

**1 vanilla pod, split lengthways and seeds scraped out**

Crumble topping

**85 g flaked almonds, toasted until lightly golden**

**85 g unsalted butter**

**115 g brown breadcrumbs**

**55 g rolled oats**

**55 g brown sugar**

*4 individual ovenproof dishes, or a shallow baking dish*

Serves 4

Cut the rhubarb into 2.5 cm pieces. Cut the ginger into thin slices, then crossways into matchsticks. Put the rhubarb, ginger, caster sugar and vanilla pod into a saucepan and cook over gentle heat until the juices run from the rhubarb and it starts to soften. Pour into the ovenproof dishes or baking dish.

To make the topping, put the almonds into a dry frying pan and cook, stirring, over gentle heat until lightly golden. Take care or they may burn. Remove and reserve.

Add the butter to the frying pan and heat gently until melted. Add the breadcrumbs, rolled oats and brown sugar. Increase the heat and cook briskly, stirring continuously, until the breadcrumbs and oats start to caramelize, brown and separate. Remove from the pan and stir in the toasted almonds.

Sprinkle the mixture over the rhubarb, starting at the edges and working towards the middle. Press down firmly. Transfer to a preheated oven and cook at 200°C (400°F) Gas 6 for about 10 minutes until the topping is crisp and golden (the forced rhubarb is very tender and will finish cooking in this time).

A berry cobbler that's equally good made with raspberries, blackberries or blueberries. Apples have their own natural sweetness, so less sugar has to be added to the filling. For a light scone topping, use your hands to shape the dough (a rolling pin is too heavy for such a light mixture). The walnuts and brown sugar become pleasingly crisp and contrast well with the airy scones.

# berry and apple crispy cobbler

**5 medium red apples**
**500 g berries**
**1 tablespoon caster sugar**

Cobbler topping
**250 g self-raising flour**
**½ teaspoon salt**
**3 teaspoon baking powder**
**1 tablespoon caster sugar**
**50 g unsalted butter, diced**
**75 ml milk mixed
with 75 ml water**
**1 egg**
**1 tablespoon single cream**
**2 tablespoons coarsely
chopped walnut pieces**
**1 tablespoon brown sugar**

To serve
**icing sugar, for dusting**
**whipped cream**

*a square or round ovenproof baking
dish, 25 cm diameter, 5 cm deep*

*a 6 cm fluted biscuit cutter*

Serves 4–6

Peel, core and thinly slice the apples. Rinse the berries and pat dry with kitchen paper. Put the apples and berries into the baking dish, sprinkle with the caster sugar and toss gently to coat the fruit in sugar.

To make the topping, sieve the flour, salt and baking powder into a mixing bowl, then stir in the caster sugar. Cut the butter into small pieces, add to the bowl and rub in with your fingertips until there are no large lumps of butter and the mixture resembles fine breadcrumbs.

Put the milk and water mixture into a bowl, add the egg, then beat well. Make a well in the flour mixture, then pour in the egg mixture. Using a table knife, draw the mixture lightly together to form a soft dough.

Turn out onto a floured work surface and quickly and lightly knead the dough until smooth. Form into a ball with the sides of your hand and press out evenly and lightly with the flat of your hand to about 1½ cm thick. Cut out 8 scones with the biscuit cutter, then arrange them down the sides or around the edge of the baking dish, on top of the fruit, leaving a space in the centre so they will cook evenly. Brush with the cream and sprinkle with the chopped walnuts and brown sugar.

Bake in a preheated oven at 220°C (425°F) Gas 7 for 5 minutes. Reduce the temperature to 200°C (400°F) Gas 6 and bake for a further 20 minutes until the scones are well risen, golden brown and crisp with a light, fluffy centre.

Dust with icing sugar and serve with whipped cream.

# sicilian almond and orange cake

6 large eggs
a pinch of salt
175 g caster sugar
finely grated zest of 1 orange
175 g plain flour, sifted twice

### Filling

750 g ricotta cheese
75 g icing sugar, sifted
125 ml Cointreau or other
orange liqueur
85 g bitter dark chocolate
(at least 55–60 per cent cocoa
solids), finely chopped
2 tablespoons shelled pistachio
nuts, blanched, peeled and
coarsely chopped
4 tablespoons blanched
almonds, coarsely chopped
5 pieces mixed candied fruits,
excess sugar washed off,
dried and coarsely chopped,
plus extra to serve

### Topping

350 ml double cream, whipped
to a soft, floppy consistency
fresh lemon leaves (optional)

*2 sandwich cake tins,
20 cm diameter, greased and
base-lined with baking parchment*

Serves 8–10

This flamboyantly flavoured cake with its beautiful topping of candied fruit is almost irresistible. To me, it is the epitome of Sicily: I love the cake almost as much as I love the island.

Put the eggs, salt and sugar into a large bowl and, using an electric mixer, whisk until the mixture doubles in volume and becomes pale and creamy. With the machine still running, gradually whisk in 2 tablespoon boiling water – the mixture will thicken considerably and increase in volume. Add the orange zest. Continue whisking until the mixture has tripled in volume and, when the whisk is lifted, the mixture leaves a ribbon-like trail on the surface.

Sprinkle half the sifted flour over the surface. Using a metal spoon, carefully and quickly fold in the flour, taking care not to break down the volume. Repeat with the remaining flour. Pour half the mixture into each prepared cake tin and bake in a preheated oven at 180°C (350°F) Gas 4 for 20–25 minutes until the sponges are golden, well risen and shrinking slightly from the edge of the tins. Transfer to a wire rack and let cool. Carefully peel off the parchment, taking care not to rip the sponge (you may need to use a palette knife to help push down the sponge).

To make the filling, put the ricotta into a bowl, then sift in the icing sugar and 3 tablespoons of the liqueur. Whisk until light and fluffy. Add the chocolate, nuts and chopped candied fruit and fold into the mixture.

To assemble, put one sponge, top side down, onto a large plate. Sprinkle 2 tablespoons liqueur over the surface and let soak for a few minutes. Spread the filling over the top. Sprinkle the underside of the second sponge with 1 tablespoon liqueur, then put on top of the filling. Finally, sprinkle the top of the cake with the remaining liqueur. Cover and chill for 2–3 hours.

To finish, spread the whipped cream over the top and sides of the cake with a palette knife. Top with the whole candied fruit pieces and lemon leaves, if using.

# chocolate truffle cake
## with caramelized pecans

This dark, smooth, meltingly rich chocolate cake is perfect for dinner parties – the smallest slice will satisfy even the grandest appetite.

**200 g dark chocolate digestive biscuits**

**90 g unsalted butter**

**125 g pecans, lightly toasted and chopped**

**30 g dark bitter chocolate (at least 55–60 per cent cocoa solids), melted**

**a pinch of ground cinnamon**

Truffle filling

**50 g pecans**

**4 heaped tablespoons icing sugar**

**600 ml double cream**

**450 g dark bitter chocolate (at least 55–60 per cent cocoa solids)**

Topping

**250 g pecan halves**

**125 g icing sugar**

**1 tablespoon cocoa powder (optional)**

*a deep, loose-based cake tin, 20 cm diameter, greased*

*a baking sheet, lightly oiled*

Serves 8–10

To make the biscuit base, put the chocolate biscuits into a blender or food processor and blend until finely crushed. Put the butter into a small saucepan and melt gently. Add the biscuit crumbs, chopped nuts, melted chocolate and cinnamon. Mix well. Pour the mixture into the prepared tin and, using the back of a spoon, firmly press down to cover the base of the tin. Chill well.

To make the filling, put the pecans into a heavy frying pan and cover with the icing sugar. Cook over a medium heat, stirring occasionally, until the sugar dissolves and turns into a deep caramel which coats the nuts. Pour onto the prepared baking sheet and let cool until hard. Break into pieces. Transfer to a food processor and blend until fine.

Put the cream into a bowl and whip until soft peaks form. Chop the chocolate, put into a heatproof bowl set over a saucepan of simmering water and melt gently. Do not let any water or steam touch the chocolate. Let cool slightly.

Fold the melted chocolate into the whipped cream until smooth, then fold in the processed caramelized nuts. Pour the mixture over the biscuit base in the prepared tin. Tap the tin on the work surface a few times to level the mixture and remove any trapped air bubbles. Cover and chill in the refrigerator for at least 4–5 hours, preferably overnight.

To make the topping, put the pecan halves into a frying pan, sprinkle over the icing sugar and caramelize, harden and cool as before. Remove the truffle cake from the tin and transfer to a serving plate. If using cocoa, sift it thickly over the top and arrange the caramelized pecans in a circle around the edge of the cake.

This very simple yet elegant cheesecake needs no fruit for embellishment. However, a few chocolate curls or 'caraques' resting on the glossy sour cream glaze look wonderful.

# baked lemon and chocolate cheesecake

300 g plain chocolate digestive biscuits

100 g unsalted butter

70 g chopped walnuts

30 g dark bitter chocolate (at least 55–60 per cent cocoa solids), finely chopped

Filling

420 g cream cheese

finely grated zest and juice of 2 lemons

1 vanilla pod, split lengthways and seeds scraped out

3 large eggs

200 g caster sugar

Topping

150 ml sour cream

a little freshly grated nutmeg

Chocolate Caraques (curls or quills)*

icing sugar, for dusting

*a loose-based flan tin, 25 cm diameter*

Serves 8

To make the biscuit base, put the chocolate biscuits into a blender or food processor and process until finely crushed.

Put the butter into a saucepan and melt over a gentle heat. Stir in the biscuit crumb mixture, chopped walnuts and chopped chocolate. Heat until melted and well mixed, about 2–3 minutes.

Pour the biscuit mixture into the flan tin and, using the back of a spoon, firmly press down to cover the base and sides of the tin evenly. Chill well.

To make the filling, put the cream cheese, lemon zest and juice and vanilla seeds into a large bowl and beat until light and smooth. Put the eggs and sugar into a separate bowl and, using an electric mixer, whisk until the mixture thickens and when the whisk is lifted the mixture leaves a ribbon-like trail on the surface. Using the whisk, gently fold the egg mixture into the cream cheese mixture, until blended but still light and fluffy. Pour into the prepared biscuit base.

Bake in a preheated oven at 140°C (275°F) Gas 1 for about 30–35 minutes until only just set: the cheesecake will continue cooking as it cools.

While the cheesecake is still slightly warm, pour the sour cream over the top of the filling – it will set and become very glossy. When the cheesecake is completely cool, sprinkle with a little freshly grated nutmeg. Top with the chocolate caraques and dust with icing sugar just before serving.

**\*Chocolate Caraques** Pour melted chocolate onto a chopping board and let set. Using a long knife, and working away from you, slowly scrape over the chocolate. The chocolate will curl into quills.

# strawberry cheesecake

This light, fruity, uncooked cheesecake is perfect for a summer's day – thanks to packaged gelatine, it is simple and easy to make.

**125 g shortbread**

**25 g unsalted butter**

Strawberry cheese filling

**600 g strawberries, washed, dried and hulled**

**grated zest and juice of ½ lemon**

**1 sachet powdered gelatine (12 g)**

**200 g cream cheese**

**4 heaped tablespoons caster sugar**

**1 vanilla pod, split lengthways and seeds scraped out**

**2 tablespoons plain yoghurt**

**150 ml double cream**

**1 large egg white**

**a pinch of salt**

**a few sprigs of mint, to serve (optional)**

*a deep loose-based cake tin, 18 cm diameter, lightly buttered*

Serves 6–8

Put the shortbread into a blender or food processor and blend until finely crushed. Melt the butter in a small saucepan. Add the shortbread crumbs and mix well. Pour the buttered crumbs into the prepared tin and, using the back of a spoon, firmly press them down to cover the base. Bake in a preheated oven at 180°C (350°) Gas 4 for 8–10 minutes, then remove from the oven and let cool.

Cut about 10 small strawberries in half and reserve for later. Put the rest into a bowl. Add the lemon zest and juice and crush lightly with a fork, making sure the strawberries are still chunky.

Put 3 tablespoons hot (but not boiling) water into a heatproof bowl, then sprinkle in the gelatine. Let stand for about 5 minutes, then put into a saucepan of water and heat gently, stirring until the gelatine completely dissolves.

Put the cream cheese into a bowl and beat until soft. Add the sugar, vanilla seeds, yoghurt and cream and beat until the mixture is smooth and fluffy. Fold in the crushed strawberry mixture.

Mix a spoonful of the strawberry cheese mixture into the gelatine to lighten it, then steadily pour back into the strawberry cheese mixture, stirring constantly as you pour, until well mixed.

Whisk the egg white and salt until stiff peaks form, then fold into the strawberry cheese mixture and pour on top of the biscuit base in the tin. Tap the tin on the work surface a few times to let the mixture settle and to level the surface. Cover and chill in the refrigerator for at least 2–3 hours until set.

To serve, turn out onto a serving plate, top with the reserved strawberries and a sprig or two of mint, if using.

# boston cream pie

A New England classic, this is really a cake, not a pie, and is usually thicker than the one I make. I think the apricot purée adds clarity and freshness, but it also isn't traditional. To make chocolate leaves, paint the underside of unsprayed rose leaves with melted chocolate and leave to cool. When completely set, carefully peel away the leaves to reveal perfect chocolate replicas.

1 tablespoon unsalted butter
75 ml milk
2 eggs
115 g caster sugar
½ teaspoon vanilla extract
75 g plain flour
1 teaspoon baking powder
a pinch of salt

Filling
425 ml milk
4 large egg yolks
1 vanilla pod, split lengthways and seeds scraped out
2 tablespoons cornflour
4 tablespoons caster sugar
3 canned apricot halves, in natural juice

Topping
100 g plain bitter chocolate (at least 55–60 per cent cocoa solids)
25 g unsalted butter
1 tablespoon strong black coffee
chocolate leaves (optional – see recipe introduction)

*a 20 cm deep round cake tin, greased, floured and base-lined with baking parchment*

Serves 6–8

To make the sponge, put the butter and milk into a small saucepan and heat gently until the butter has melted. Keep the mixture warm.

Using an electric mixer, whisk the eggs, sugar and vanilla in a large bowl until pale, thick and creamy and the mixture leaves a ribbon-like trail when the whisk is lifted. Sift the flour, baking powder and salt over the mixture in 2 batches. Using a large metal spoon, fold in the first batch, then the second.

Trickle the warmed butter and milk mixture around the edge of the sponge mixture, near the sides of the bowl, then gently fold in to make a smooth batter. Pour into the prepared tin and bake in a preheated oven at 180°C (350°F) Gas 4 for 25–30 minutes until well risen, the sponge has shrunk slightly from the sides and a skewer inserted in the middle comes out clean.

Let cool in the tin for 5 minutes, then turn out onto a wire rack and let cool completely. Peel off the baking parchment and slice the cake into 2 layers.

To make the filling, put the milk into a saucepan and slowly bring it to the boil. Put the egg yolks, vanilla seeds, cornflour and sugar into a bowl, mix well, then whisk into the hot milk. Strain the mixture, then pour back into the pan and return to the heat. Simmer gently for 3–4 minutes, whisking vigorously until smooth and thick. Remove, put clingfilm over the surface to prevent a skin forming and let cool. Chill.

Put the apricots into a blender and work to a purée, adding a little juice from the can to loosen the mixture if necessary.

To make the topping, melt the chocolate, butter and coffee in a heatproof bowl set over a saucepan of simmering water. Mix until glossy and smooth.

To assemble the cake, put one sponge layer on a serving plate and spread the filling on top, up to the edges. Dot 3 tablespoons of the apricot purée over the filling and swirl with the tip of a small knife.

Put the second sponge layer on top of the filling. Spread the chocolate topping over the sandwiched cake, chill until almost set, then add the chocolate leaves, if using, and serve.

The taste and texture of this beautiful cake actually improve over a day or two, as the flavours develop and intensify. If you can't find framboise (raspberry liqueur), try Kirsch instead.

# rich chocolate cake
## with raspberries and framboise cream

125 g dark bitter chocolate (at least 55–60 per cent cocoa solids), chopped

50 ml dark rum

4 large eggs, separated

125 g caster sugar, plus extra for sprinkling

a pinch of salt

Raspberry filling

600 ml double cream

1 tablespoon caster sugar

2 tablespoons framboise (raspberry liqueur) or Kirsch

500 g raspberries

icing sugar, for dusting

tiny sprigs of mint, to serve

*3 round sandwich tins, 20 cm diameter, greased and base-lined with baking parchment*

*greaseproof paper*

Serves 8–10

Put the chocolate and rum into a heatproof bowl set over a saucepan of simmering water and heat until melted.

Put the egg yolks and sugar into a large bowl and, using an electric mixer, whisk until the mixture doubles in volume, becomes thick and creamy and leaves a ribbon-like trail on the surface when the whisk is lifted. Fold in the melted rum and chocolate mixture.

Put the egg whites and salt into a bowl and whisk until stiff peaks form.

Gently fold into the chocolate mixture, a third at a time, taking care not to break down the volume of the mixture. Divide the mixture evenly between the prepared tins and bake in a preheated oven at 180°C (350°F) Gas 4 for 15–20 minutes until risen, the sponge has shrunk slightly from the sides and a skewer inserted in the middle comes out clean. The cakes will have a cracked surface.

Lay large sheets of greaseproof paper on 2 wire cooling racks and sprinkle with a thin layer of caster sugar. Turn out the cakes onto the sugared greaseproof paper and let cool.

To make the filling, put the cream, sugar and framboise into a bowl and lightly whip until soft peaks form. Reserve about 100 g of the raspberries, then gently fold the rest into the whipped cream.

Sandwich the raspberry cream filling evenly between the 3 chocolate sponges to make a layered cake. Top with the reserved raspberries. Sift icing sugar over the raspberries and the cake, then add sprigs of mint and serve.

jellies, soufflés
and meringues

# hazelnut lemon meringue cake

This lovely, chewy, nutty-flavoured meringue is very easy to make. Don't over-grind the hazelnuts, as this releases the nut oils and makes the meringue heavy. Making lemon curd is a good way of using the spare yolks from this cake and the sharp lemony flavour marries particularly well with the sweetness of the meringue. Extra yolks have many uses.

**6 large egg whites**

**a pinch of salt**

**450 g caster sugar**

**115 g skinned hazelnuts, toasted in a dry frying pan, then coarsely ground**

**250–300 ml double cream, lightly whipped to soft peaks**

**6–8 tablespoons Lemon Curd (see page 62)**

**1 tablespoon icing sugar, for dusting**

*2 baking sheets, lined with baking parchment and marked with a 20 cm circle*

*long metal skewers*

Serves 8–10

Put the egg whites and salt into a large, clean, grease free bowl and whisk with an electric mixer until soft peaks form. Using a large metal spoon, fold in one-third of the sugar. Whisk again until glossy and stiff. Repeat once more with the remaining sugar.

Sprinkle the ground hazelnuts over the top, then carefully and lightly fold into the meringue – take care not to break down the volume of the mixture.

Divide the nut meringue between the 2 prepared trays and spread the mixture to fill each marked circle.

Bake in a preheated oven at 170°C (325°F) Gas 3 for about 1¼–1½ hours, swapping the trays halfway through cooking, until crisp on the outside and soft in the middle. Remove from the oven and let cool. Alternatively, for a crisper meringue, switch off the oven and leave the meringues inside for about 2 hours, then remove. When completely cold, carefully peel off the baking parchment and put one meringue onto a serving plate. Spread the whipped cream over the top, then the lemon curd. Top with the second meringue, set upside down.

Sift the icing sugar over the top of the layered meringue. Heat several long metal skewers until red hot, then use to make crisscross patterns on top: the heat from the skewers will caramelize the sugar.

# chocolate and tia maria soufflé

225 g bitter chocolate, chopped

2 tablespoons coffee liqueur

4 large egg whites

a pinch of salt

4 tablespoons caster sugar

icing sugar, for dusting

*4 soufflé dishes, 125 ml each,*
*about 8 cm diameter,*
*lightly greased and dusted*
*with caster sugar*

Serves 4

Gently melt the chocolate in a heatproof bowl set over a saucepan of simmering water, stirring with a spatula. Let cool a little – it must be liquid when added to the egg whites. Pour 1 tablespoon of the chocolate and ½ tablespoon of the coffee liqueur into each soufflé dish.

Put the egg whites and salt into a large, clean, grease free bowl and whisk until stiff. Add 1 teaspoon of the sugar and whisk until glossy and stiff. Add half the remaining sugar and whisk back to stiff peaks. Repeat with the remaining sugar. Using a whisk, gently and quickly fold the melted chocolate into the whites. Pour the mixture into the soufflé dishes and bake immediately in a preheated oven at 225°C (425°F) Gas 7 for 4–5 minutes until well risen and crusty on top. Dust lightly with icing sugar and serve immediately.

# apricot and orange soufflé

Coarsely chop 3 of the apricots and divide between the prepared soufflé dishes. Finely grate the orange zest and divide half between the soufflé dishes.

Put the remaining apricots and orange zest into a blender or food processor. Add the egg yolks, vanilla seeds, cream, lemon juice, sugar and flour. Purée until smooth.

Put the egg whites into a large, clean, grease free bowl. Using an electric hand-held mixer, whisk until soft peaks form. Sift the cream of tartar on top and whisk again until stiff peaks form. Using a large metal spoon, fold the purée into the beaten egg whites, taking care not to break down the volume. Pour into the prepared dishes. Run your thumb around the inside edge of each dish.

Bake in a preheated oven at 200°C (400°F) Gas 6 for 10–12 minutes, until the soufflés are well risen and golden brown. Dust with icing sugar and serve.

410 g canned apricots in natural juice, well drained

2 oranges

3 eggs, separated

seeds from 1 split vanilla pod

2 tablespoons double cream

1 teaspoon freshly squeezed lemon juice

2 tablespoons sugar

2 tablespoons plain flour

½ teaspoon cream of tartar

icing sugar, for dusting

*6 soufflé dishes, 8 cm diameter,*
*prepared as in the previous recipe*

Serves 6

Preparing soufflés need not be intimidating – just make sure that the transition from the mixing bowl to the dining table is smooth and without interruption. Serve as soon as they come out of the oven.

# strawberry and vanilla fool

Fools are easy and delicious puddings. You can use any soft fruit – or even crisp ones, if you cook them to to a soft purée first.

500 g strawberries

2 tablespoons icing sugar

1 vanilla pod, split lengthways and seeds scraped out

225 ml double cream

2 teaspoons vanilla icing sugar (see note page 4) or icing sugar

½ recipe Quick Vanilla Custard, using 3 egg yolks, well chilled (page 62)

*6 glasses*

Serves 6

Reserve a few small strawberries for serving. Put the rest into a blender or food processor, add the icing sugar, blend to a purée, then pour into a bowl. Add the vanilla pod and seeds to the strawberry mixture and chill for an hour or so to infuse. Press through a fine nylon sieve to make a smooth, thick purée.

Put the cream and vanilla sugar into a bowl. Whisk until thick and floppy. Chill.

To serve, fill the serving glasses with alternate layers of vanilla custard, strawberry purée and vanilla cream. Swirl together using a cocktail stick, skewer or small pointed knife to give a marbled effect. Cut the reserved strawberries in half, add to the glasses, then serve chilled.

# raspberry cranachan

A traditional Scottish pudding using local ingredients – whisky, heather honey, raspberries and oatmeal.

Put the oatmeal into a dry frying pan and toast gently until dry. Add the sugar and continue toasting until the oatmeal is golden and caramelized. Let cool.

Put the cream and honey into a bowl, whisk until thick, then fold in the whisky. Set aside a few small, perfect raspberries for serving. Fold the remainder into the cream mixture, then taste and add a little more honey if needed.

Layer the whisky raspberry cream in glasses in alternate layers with the crunchy oatmeal. Top with the reserved raspberries and serve well chilled.

55 g coarse oatmeal

1 tablespoon brown sugar

300 ml double cream

1 tablespoon light honey

4–5 tablespoons malt whisky

175 g fresh raspberries or tayberries, about 1 punnet

*6 glasses*

Serves 6

To produce a crystal clear, shimmering jelly, it is important to use leaf gelatine: happily, it is also simplicity itself to handle. To be truly sophisticated, worthy of any smart dinner party, the jelly must be light and wobbly without a trace of stiffness.

# blackberry and port jelly
## with vanilla and port syrup

**250 g fresh blackberries**
**125 g caster sugar**
**juice of ½ lemon**
**150 ml late-bottled vintage port**
**4 thin sheets of leaf gelatine**

Vanilla and port syrup
**125 g caster sugar**
**1 vanilla pod, split lengthways and seeds scraped out**
**3 large fresh blackberries**

To serve
**a few blackberries**
**icing sugar, for dusting**
**4–6 sprigs of mint (optional)**

*4–6 individual moulds, wetted with water – simple shapes work best, such as small ramekins or pudding tins*

Serves 4–6

To make the jelly, put the blackberries into a saucepan, add 300 ml cold water, the sugar, lemon juice and port, bring to the boil and simmer gently until tender. Press through a nylon sieve to remove all the seeds.

Put the leaf gelatine into a bowl and cover with cold water. Leave for 10 minutes to soften, then drain and squeeze the leaves with your hand to remove excess water before stirring them into the warm fruit liquid. Stir until completely dissolved. Pour the mixture into the wetted moulds and let set in the refrigerator.

To make the syrup, put 100 ml water into a saucepan, add the sugar and dissolve over a low heat. Increase the heat and bring to the boil. Add the split vanilla pod and blackberries and simmer until reduced by half to make a thick syrup. Press through a fine nylon sieve, pushing through the blackberry flesh, but retaining the seeds and vanilla pod in the sieve. (You will now have a pink blush-coloured syrup flavoured heavily with vanilla.) Chill well.

When ready to serve, dip the base of the moulds very briefly in hot water and turn out the jellies onto serving plates. Top with a pile of berries, a pool of vanilla syrup, a light dusting of icing sugar and a sprig of mint, if using.

A pinch of salt added to the egg whites increases the volume and stabilizes the foam, so the meringue holds its shape better, while the combination of lemon juice, cornflour and sugar gives the meringue a thick marshmallow centre, so typical of pavlova. The sweetness of the meringue is offset by the sharpness of the fruit. In Australia, the home of pavlova, other fruits are used, such as strawberries and tropical fruit, so feel free to vary the recipe using whatever is sweet and ripe – and in season. Passionfruit, however, is almost mandatory.

# raspberry and passionfruit pavlova

4 large egg whites
a pinch of salt
375 g caster sugar
1 tablespoon sugar
1 tablespoon cornflour
2 teaspoons freshly squeezed lemon juice

Filling

300 ml double cream
300 g raspberries
3–4 passionfruit

Raspberry purée (optional)

300 g raspberries
1–2 tablespoons icing sugar, sifted

*a baking sheet, lined with baking parchment and sprinkled with cornflour*

Serves 6–8

Put the egg whites and salt into a large bowl. Using an electric mixer, whisk the egg whites until stiff. Gradually add two-thirds of the caster sugar, whisking between each addition until the meringue is very glossy and stiff. Whisk in the remaining caster sugar.

Sift the sugar and cornflour together into a small bowl and mix well. Fold half the cornflour mixture into the meringue, then 1 teaspoon of the lemon juice. Repeat.

Spoon half the meringue onto the baking parchment and spread out to a disc about 18 cm diameter. Smooth the top and sides. Spoon the rest of the meringue in a ring around the edge of the circle of meringue until the pavlova is about 6 cm thick.

Bake in a preheated oven at 120°C (250°F) Gas ½ for about 1–1¼ hours. Remove from the oven and let cool. Alternatively, switch off the oven and leave the meringue inside until cool. This will help reduce cracking.

To make the raspberry purée, crush the raspberries with a fork or hand-held stick blender, then press through a nylon sieve to make a purée. Discard the seeds. Mix in enough of the icing sugar to sweeten to taste.

When the pavlova is cold, carefully remove the baking parchment and put the pavlova onto a serving plate. Fill the centre with the whipped cream and top with the raspberries. Cut the passionfruit in half and scoop out the pulp and seeds onto the raspberries. Serve decorated with a few sprigs of mint and the raspberry purée.

# basic recipes

## lemon curd

Unwaxed lemons are best for recipes using lemon zest, but, if you can't find them, soak the lemons in very hot water first to melt the wax, then dry thoroughly before starting on the recipe.

**finely grated zest and juice
of 3 unwaxed lemons
125 g unsalted butter
125 g caster sugar
6 large egg yolks, beaten**

Makes about 500 ml

Put the lemon zest, juice and butter into a heatproof bowl set over a saucepan of simmering water or in the top of a double boiler. Heat gently until the butter has melted and the sugar has dissolved.

Remove from the heat, add the beaten egg yolks and mix well. Return to the heat and cook gently, stirring constantly until thickened. The curd should be thick enough to coat the back of a spoon and leave a trail when lifted.

Pass through a fine sieve to remove any bits of zest or lemon pulp. Use to fill meringues, cakes or sandwiches or, alternatively, pour into a sterilized jar (see page 4) and refrigerate until needed. Use within 1 month.

## quick vanilla custard

Using cornflour to stabilize custard may not please the purists, but it works perfectly and prevents any possibility of curdling.

**5 egg yolks
1 teaspoon cornflour
2 tablespoons caster sugar
1 vanilla pod
600 ml double cream**

Serves 4–6

Put the egg yolks, cornflour and sugar into a mixing bowl and whisk well.

Split the vanilla pod lengthways and scrape out the seeds. Put the seeds and the cream into a saucepan and bring to the boil. When the cream rises in the pan, quickly pour it onto the egg mixture, whisking vigorously and continuously until the custard thickens.

# old vic foolproof pastry

This pastry is named after my restaurant, the Old Vicarage. It is used in a number of the recipes in this book. You can't go wrong with it, provided you follow the method exactly.

**1 egg**
**1 teaspoon freshly squeezed lemon juice**
**175 g plain flour**
**a pinch of salt**
**1 teaspoon icing sugar**
**120 g unsalted butter, diced**

*foil and baking beans or uncooked rice*

Makes about 330 g
(see note below right)

Put the egg and lemon juice into a bowl, add 2 tablespoons iced water and beat well. Chill until needed – the mixture will thicken slightly.

Sift the flour, salt and icing sugar into a mixing bowl. Add the butter and rub in with your fingertips until the mixture is crumbly but rough. Don't try to rub it in finely at this stage. Make a well in the centre and add the egg liquid. Using a round-bladed knife, bring the mixture together to form a dough. (Use a cutting action rather than a stirring action or the pastry will become tough when cooked.)

Transfer to a lightly floured surface and knead briefly until the dough is smooth, like putty. Wrap in clingfilm and let rest in the refrigerator for at least 30 minutes before using. Roll out to a shape just larger than the pie plate or tart tin you will be using.

**Baking Blind** If the recipe tells you to bake the pastry blind, after rolling out the pastry, use the rolling pin to help you lift the pastry and carefully lower it into the tart tin. Ease it evenly up the sides of the tin, taking care not to trap air between the pastry and the tin. Take particular care where the sides meet the base. Prick the base of the pastry with a fork.

Line with foil and fill with baking beans or uncooked rice. Bake in a preheated oven at 180°C (350°F) Gas 4 for 15 minutes. Remove the foil and beans and return the pastry case to the oven for a further 5 minutes to dry out and cook through. Fill as described in the recipe chosen.

**Pastry Quantity** The quantity of pastry given here is enough for one large tart, 20 cm diameter, or 6 tartlets, 10 cm diameter. For a deep, double-crusted pie, 25 cm diameter, such as the Old Fashioned Apple Pie on page 19, double the ingredients. There is no need to make two separate batches.

# index